CW00524220

FIONA WAS HERE

poetry to live with

Irene Cunningham

All proceeds to Breast Cancer UK

Cover design by the author;
original image from the family

Other publications

FAIRYTALE
(Collected Poems)

Writing in partnership with Diana Devlin

SANDMEN: A Space Odyssey
(a conversation in poetry)

HALLOWEEN
(Seasonal poetry & prose)

Dedicated to The Edmistons, old and new, the McGovern family, and Joe, with forever love.

Memory is art
set to the music of time.

CONTENTS

FI

She'd say, *Thanks Doll*,
nibble the edges of toast
to show willing,
ooh and aah at chocolate,
discuss fig rolls and Garibaldi.
Her body had her pinned
like a 17th century witch
with a weighted door on her chest.
Not even a spoonful of sugar
helped the food go down;
she smiled, we ate and she melted
into our terrified love.

UPHEAVAL

My neck displays age in its new wattle.
In years to come Dystopia might sing
the blues, recall echoes of *Godzilla*
on city towers. I may be monstrous –
everything consumed, compacted, swallowed.
Time is a hungry beast, a new spring lamb;
children magicked into adults. As light
drifts off to bed I'll think about hefting
home to write lists, tick off dancing, drama,
cook all the veg in the fridge; make great soup.
If a dragon roars out of my fireplace
I'll invite it to dinner, offer toast
and apologise for the lack of plump
young flesh...stress my unappetising frame.

GREEN LIGHTS

Her wig came today.
She posted a pic on *FB*,
a whole life in her eyes.

I flip back in my head;
she's fifteen again – funny
how people remain intact.

Thirty-five years hunker
in that space; I re-invented
myself, left her to live.

In the last twenty years…
a bleeding brain, five funerals,
two weddings and big birthdays

drove us together. Now
we're scrolling for news
as she walks the wards

sucks up the poison, waits
at junctions where emeralds
scatter the path ahead.

BODY LANGUAGE

Who goes there, reflecting
versions of itself into soft
tissue disguising to confuse?

I look in mirrors, twist to feel
what's going on inside, imagine
a map of me but can't see through

all this skin and blood; more
tests are formulating, waiting.
If only I could slip a hand in

to get the picture – I think I could
be blind, use my hands to know.
Am I built the same as other women?

My parts feel like a generic jigsaw.
Can a body be suicidal, demand
torture? It's keeping its guilty secrets

and even the creaking is silent.

MARCH QUICKENING

I'm thinking of running a rake
through clumped grass, comb it out,
untangle last season's dead, make way
for machinery.

Windswept moor...I'm Cathy calling
for Heathcliffe but I'd only want to use
his muscle. Spring is a chore.

Now I must fish my son off a river
to pilot a mower before the grass turns hippy.

I'm spending time making shapes
to drape across these old shoulders,
have visions of me in floppy hat in the sun,
clasping wool at my neck.

I want to sail this house like a Chinese
boat into eccentric waters, dozing,
wearing trailing skirts and ruby slippers.

Brisk Involvement in Spring

Thou shalt hasten to *Aldi*, purchase, melons
and blueberries, oranges and broccoli...
acquire an exercise bike from *Amazon.*

Mince into *Iceland*, buy beans, celery
and chicken, tomatoes and garlic and
crock a pot full of ready meals, steel

yourself in a cage where time's lost,
fall into a long book, let it keep you
for a week; hold mindlessness high.

Mind the gap when falling from habits;
there's danger from accidental suicide
and overenthusiastic amelioration.

Consider the bluebells; Easter-wrapped
chocolate in April will arrest you – ride
the bike. May fortune sway your browser

from motiveless activities, exercise care
in your choice of adventures, impulses;
reverse away from cliff edges, chasms.

Parts of you will rot with the camellias
and you'll walk a petal-strewn path,
down the summer of revolution, elope

with yourself; the changing dimensions
for the coffin will save a fortune, and
shoulder-stress on ushers. Move your ass

out of discontenting winter...don't marry
the fat of the land for it doesn't dream
of you, only reaching the free air above.

From 8th July

I'm always stunned to see age
on a face I haven't seen for years.
This Fiona, bald head, bold-framed
glasses holding fierce, laughing eyes...
determined to stand, show strength.

Inside my head she's a teenager.

Even as she sleeps cells bustle as if
a deadline demands to show off how far
they've come in a six month rampage.

Shrunk, cut out from the first murder
attempt, the secondary will succeed.
They can clock off, satisfaction guaranteed.

I'm Looking Through You

Scraps of life scream
at empty spaces, fools on hills,
dreamers watching rainbows,
waiting for the magical mystery tour.

Man: humans in a different world
who won't know life before the end…
that we were across a universe

eating cake, fattening complicit bones.

Gone from this blue place
generations must metamorphose –
our genes get a ticket to ride,
travelling the long and winding road.

In my life, songs remind us
of revolution; right here we die.
Earth's political pandemic plagues us,
spreads pandemonium…ill will.

I live in a pocket, carry that weight.

NO FRONTIER

Fortnite by fortnight
years bleed into intoxication –
there's no time to think
of work or working
on a dream.
This life's a game.
Hoi Polloi bench their minds
on the bottom layer
busy in a digital frame
that binds, hypnotises.
Blood into pixels
eyes swerved
in tunnel vision.
Distraction is robbery.
Survival means choosing
abilities for power
emulating pilots
in a flight simulator.
They've fallen in love –
animation without living
the blood and guts
of an untidy world.

HOME

Inside my skull, the meat is all bustle –
a viral market-place frizzling in anticipation.

Under the dome roof my eyes relax,
swim in dreams that sparkle, fractions –

they know there's no straight path between
A and B...it's all bloody algebra. See the lake

of possibilities? Me in a little boat, rowing,
sculling like a professional...technology, light.

Cave-space, perspective – this head is different
from my face in the mirror. Familiar territory,

remembrances that flutter while I walk,
disappear my time into anthologies, sometimes

little novellas burrowing deep to discover
secret knowledge. Old age whispers a song

and we dance to *Getting to know you...*

The Weight of Ghosts

My grandmother is
a frail fairytale. I must
trust to memory
wisps of butter-coloured hair.
I should have driven
deep in my mind the loved lines
of her face as well
as the map of my Glasgow,
marked her smile instead
of memorable music.
When she existed
God and religion were an
extension of her
old age pension. Nuns
followed her home. She hassled
priests and wandered streets
in the middle of the night
wrapped up tight in tweed
searching for a sister lost
in time. Now my hair
is wound up with sliding ghosts
her combs curl, gouging
Tortoiseshell teeth in my scalp.
Bone spears through leather.
I float past security
at airports, alive
and dead, unremarkable.
As long as I live
she'll feel the wind in my hair.

THE NEWS

Yellow is interfering
closing doors devilishly
switching her off.

INSOMNIA

I snooze like a naked old bear,
rumble and turn; the heating sits
at 16, house clicks, floorboards whisper.

Bookshelves smother walls and hundreds
of tales idle their napping life away
until I die or choose them.

It would take days to clear my obsessions,
peel me from these two rooms. But if
I lived in doorways with only traffic

carrying a city home from pubs, clubs,
carpeted halls, to lull me to sleep
I'd hear kissed goodnights, promises waved

at lamplit windows, drunks laughing.
I'd be curled on cardboard, a sleeping
bag merging into dystopian fiction.

SECRET GARDENS

Movement in time blurs the speed
of light; my eyes can't keep up with the past.

I'll stand ever the hero, fly into battle
grab leaves and grain here, mushrooms

there. Hear the music, solid as oak trees,
like rented witchcraft spelling out reality,

settling old stories in new plans, underpinning
foundations. Grate skin from your knuckles

into soup – this magical anarchy is sensible
sensibility, honesty that's godly, whole

as pale cabbage, packed tight, white at heart.
Courage is crisp, straight as a javelin.

From 9th July
SHINY GIRL

She wore the bloom today,
surprised her doctor with leaps
in measurements – an un-gunged liver.
All hail the steroids.

Is it the apex? A gorge may appear
beneath us, eat her up in one sitting
though weeks were whispered,
a spark was born – immunotherapy
hovers, trembles on our lips.

DONOR

How many mothers make a day
for themselves
create space
fictions
poetry from battles
and bottle the blood?

I have vintage years
in recesses
stacked against plain plonk.

Capsules of me donated daily
dispensed with stress
and forgetfulness
gleaming
dark like beads
of death.

So when my day comes
crack open my skull
feel the suction
of fresh kill
slap it on a slab
slice sensible cuts
with intelligent hardware –
a cuisine challenge.

Marinade my thoughts
barbecue scattered dreams
pull away the gristle
and fry my age-old brain
with herby garlic mushroom;
I am nothing
if not useful.

PAPER-TRAIL

People-watching with photographs, flicking
through strangers, catching them cold, in actions.
Life mingling in lives long gone fills spaces,
holds building blocks together, paints pictures,
decorates now with then, fact and fiction
lost in time. Is a tear a rolling sphere,
a ball of instant knowledge exposing
you to all? Do they see behind the wall
the effort I've made to stop exploding?
Should I let them process me up that aisle
like a captured bride or let medical
students handle parts that no one has touched
in years? Dead grandmother dancing, pressing
flesh in hallowed halls – rare commodity.

BEING HERE

I asked her for a dream,
set confusion on the table
instead of entertaining punchlines.

Last night, I said, I dreamed
I had a baby – not one I'd birthed
that I could remember in the dream
but a tiny creature I held cupped
in my hands – surprise was key.

I think she's unconscious
a lot, can't remember where dreams
live or how to net them to fill
astonishment in the morning.

My dream baby was lost;
I left it somewhere, spent the dream
wondering where it had gone
how I could leave it like a purse
on a bus or a supermarket counter.

It haunted me for days, hovered
as if crying, *Why did you forget me?*
But I haven't. It may have been a boy,
a quiet, contented little thing,
just satisfied to be in the world.

Cutting my grass, soaked
in achievement I felt as if I'd fitted
a neat carpet edge to edge
while a blue sky dragged the birds
elsewhere to keep the peace.

The baby was somewhere near

not pressuring me just there
to remind me to look
where I leave my people
before they too disappear.

EDINBURGH WAVERLEY

Time slips from attosecond to minutes.
I misuse its measurements
think half-hours can be slipped into just a sec –
cancellations are nothing to me.
Shadows of girdered glass force lines upon tiles
flash dark little movies of hopeful passengers
and pigeons. Time knows about clocks,
their movements: the fastest lasers' pulse-time
is a femosecond – language from another
dimension tickles my tongue.

Spring nods at us. The sun peers down.
Policemen stroll in pocket-fronted vests –
noticeable neon inactive. Kilted men
draw eyes. Platform boots, strappy sandals,
super-smooth 4-wheeled cases,
tartan trews, blaring scarlet trousers
and a Gothic coat pass my time.

Time speaks Bell, understands Alarm,
I see it in crocheted blankets,
diaries, photo albums, on film, in fossils,
pressed flowers, poems.

White shirt with tartan bow-tie and skinny jeans
escorts tottering Cinderella in her glass
fuck-me high-heels – at this time in the day!
I suffered the sight of an ugly shell-suit jacket
in a hurry...know that this is how my friends
will dress me on my last journey.
I wonder at a new career
as a personal shopper to save the world.

Common years leap,

Olympiad cup themselves...Time shapes decades over Jubilees and down centuries into millennia. Done.

THE POWERS THAT BE

They're decorating the morgue
in purples; new schemes
to rescue regions, beautify –
colour raises the dead.

Dipping chicken nuggets
in barbecue sauce I ogle
the sweating actions of men at work.
Pretty men gladden the eye...

not a lust-fest; appreciation
of a stunning flower in a bed of ordinary.
This fast food haven is minimalist,
digitised. The ravenous ponder

boards, touch screens, wait
until their number's up. Only
the ancient lean on counters,
talk to humans, handle transactions.

THE ROAD TO AWE

Is not smooth but crumbles underfoot
with temporary repairs – I've just seen
a magic machine work wonders in Australia
plugging potholes with aplomb and mind-bending
simplicity. I took my hat off, am full of great
expectations...can hear my stomach rumbling
but impressive cake is nowhere to be found at 3am.
Determined rain keeps us green
enough to boast our Scottish beauty
and my tree shall be freshness incarnate
tomorrow, or the next day...or the day after.
In my sphere nothing but renegade buses
can harm me and I am always careful
in the physical world – walk don't run,
glide as if you're on a moving walkway
at the airport; arrival is assured.
Far away in the Westminster ghetto
shenanigans are hot-to-trot but nothing
to do with me in my little ant-house
and all its bills settled like syrup
quietly easing into corners to sweeten
the stress of having no ice-cream
in the freezer when summer is landing.
Minute by minute I feel happiness
on the edge of my time; it's lacy
like regency ruffles on royal cuffs
where lazy and elegant hands produce
silk handkerchiefs soaked in scent
to dismiss the smells of poverty
and raw sewage. Our concrete is clean,
rivers thoroughly diluted with luxury
rainwater falling free from our mostly
white skies. How lucky we are to be so far
from the world of cities; our skirts stick out

like paper nylon petticoats under frilly
dresses. We're all set for summer
with new white socks and sandals
to show off our good upbringing
and perfect manners – in general.
I sit in my freshly-mown garden in peace
look out at my usually quiet street
day and night and thank serendipity
for catching me in such an awesome net.

BORN TOO LATE

I woulda been a babe, a real dollface
hot mamma whose dish could sink ships to place
a sailor in my path...and he'd take me
to make whoopee, blow his horn and fill me
full of giggle-juice, thinking, *What a dame!*
No gold-digging on my mind just a swell
night to knacker the peepers in snazzy
style – time off rot-gut booze in beat clip-joints.
I woulda been a contender; aces
in this corner, sneaky keen to rise to
cool-cat; I'd be where it's at – no kiss-off
for this looker. I'd be, *Look at me Ma,*
top of the world...Patsy done good so don't
blow your wig 'cause I'll be home late tonight.

RECOVERY

They've cut and padded,
made you as comfortable as likely,
sleep eating time
like a never-ending family meal.

Everything comes
to an end and is changed.

You were fuel in a raging fire
gasping for oxygen
before the flame died...
and it was enough.

Death will be back.
Perhaps an unrestrained bus
or a spin down stairs
or brain-rot.

When you wake, ignore
If not now, when?

* * *

The invader had a baby;
a big fat cuckoo
fucked everything up.

ON CLEAR DAYS

The women behind me left a pattern.
I have five years to reach it, bridge it,
crochet time, shape-shift this self
while it lives with the bones.
In this sofa era, soft bodies sink
into architecture, stretch possibilities.
I like the stillness of coffins,
the silken sheen surround-sound.

I've lost reckless days, drunken nights
to sensible thoughts; paper calls me
the bearer. *The wolf is at the door*,
everything's illuminated. Money
has an aura. Mine has this silvery sheen
as if attainment passed angelic inspection.
I worry about news I've ignored
to live in peace with piped-in drama.

The bus raises me above milling crowds
who don't see me – to me they're flotsam.
It's diverting, hovering at bus stops
learning how to live in the last days.
The race is on. Governmental bodies
bicker to counter old promises to bear
pensions, carry ancients to their ends…
suggest we work forever, force strokes.

On clear days, we think we see the end.

WHISKY THOUGHTS

Brains are pale grey...we're all the same
colour, though stupid might be shades
of yellow/orange. Remember when

Shirley Bassey sang *If I ruled the world*,
belting out that what-if in the sixties
in her sparkling dresses, spreading fancy

while Vietnam hosted desolation?
Britain watched black&white TV, *I Love
Lucy, Rhoda, Come Dancing*, distanced,

busy preparing the metric-shoogle,
grabbing some American colour on
Top of the Pops. So, who's fit for the post...

tests if the grey matter's present?
Apparently it's assumed but later reported
missing – not in action, just disappeared.

What post? Presidential, Ministerial...
Soap-box Tenors, Tyrants & Toe-rags,
the diabolical-wish-merchants-in-drag.

If I ruled the world I couldn't trust even
a woman because the heart of darkness
lives in all the houses and humans flail

against rip tides and sucking black holes
packed with moneyed eels who don't sing
out loud, or whisper in speech bubbles.

What colour is sense and honesty...how

do they survive when madmen whip
colours into mud? Catch the bloody eels,

feed them to polar bears. There will be
no days of wine and roses, but nothing
to stop us singing, with whisky in the jar.

WAITING FOR NEWS

Listening to
Interview with a Vampire
tucking in
to double egg n chips
in a gluttonous hurry
before bad news chokes
the golden fries dipped in yolk
and I'd forever remember
their remains
congealing.

A thunder storm
crumples the day,
torrential bursts of rain
floods the street…
cars hiss through it.
Vampires exchange blood,
drag life back and forth
but only death
results.

WANTED: New Day

Applicants will be tested for depression,
rain and wind-speed – only the best
degrees need apply. No tornadoes please.
Sunny disposition an advantage.

Let the new day seep through clouds
and present itself smartly dressed, for interview.
We aim to beat the years that race away
like sprinters, leaving us lounging
in coffee shops people-watching.

Old days twist themselves in our hair
bring us together, a froth of gossip with latte.
Heart to heart we open up compartments
scan interiors for crumbs to grind our gums.
The past has worn us out.

Don't worry about mind-readers – no one
can catch your shame; it's in-growing, a verruca.
The past is a plague, bear it no mind;
really, dementia might be a gift.

GOING GENTLY

This body has softened, like my eyesight...
and these pillows will never be crisp again.
Time will disassemble me.
I won't be hour-glass shaped though
the way ahead is laced like a corset.

When I was the girl on the sideboard
Wings and *Elton John* snuggled around couples
on stairs, mingled with tart smoke...men ran
their navels across the face of my knees,
breathed cider and beer into my friendly breasts,
told me my ankles were hypnotic.
I'd throw them around, watch eyebrows twitch.

We flitted from man to man, all of us
wet terracotta, ripe with the wanting.
I became a *Rubens* woman, reclining most of the day:
not shaping my face with make-up or moulding
this torso into finer lines. I was an adventure
to tantalise a *Conan-Doyle*-mind, challenge
a psychic. Myriad thrillers, pot-boilers, tragedies
tucked in voluptuous curves of my life...
and at least one farce.

Now, I'm a range of mountains, shifting hills,
smooth lawn running down to water, a garden
of dreams. Fairies live, in my trees,
Sundays remind me of men in my bed.
I'm too young to have my own cat – still
mobile which can't be confused with nubile.

NOW

You don't have to cross-match, test the air, heave
to breathe; it's still free and clear – polluted,
but no one notices that in places like this
with hills rising behind our heads. I think
of all the *last times*, gather them like bluebells
because every day is countable. A line
of new firsts is pushing at my intentions.

An hour ago, there was home-made cake.
In the morning, first thing, will be the weighing
of the old me. Ha. Last lie passes the baton
to first deed, which will be the wearing of the will.
I dream of that space, weeks, months, ahead
where my body simpers into sighs
but that's not now: it's when I wake up.

Poor but roofed I watch my neighbours,
how they wander into their older age, safe
as ganders, padding to the local shop for talk
and bread where sense and sensibility are offered.
Health is a modern issue and eyes saunter
around the heftier people. My ancient bones
are preparing for the loss of me.

CRAFTING

The swans are coming, boasting up the river.
Seagulls on the wing curve themselves
across the blue...one swan's a-grooming.

I'm haunted by a cancerous liver – not
in my body – multiplying, a knitter perpetually
casting on extra stitches every row.

It sneaked down there from the breast, moved in
like a conqueror with pregnant wives.
Why invade to commit murder-suicide?

Up in the Scottish blue a pale crescent moon
is almost invisible. Life on the river is still at noon.
Days off float about all day to die at the end.

I'm going home to construct a Golem –
not from clay or rock; destruction is key.
Any old rubbish will do to simulate Death:

the cat's litter tray, kitchen floor sweepings,
old rags...I should search windowsills for dead
flies and moths to form the figure, paste images

of politicians on top, bring the present to bear –
there can be no panacea but there must be
a burning. Live for a day to know life.

LOOKING FOR ANGELA CARTER

Did she leave a map?
Magic is tricky.
I'm waiting
for something to switch on or off
edge me into giantism
stretch me thin to tower,
stride, get anywhere soon.

These bones are weighed down,
multiple voices bore into my brain.
Distal phalanges dance like old-time
pianola keys...want to be longer
to play more than *Chopsticks*.

I'm a five-foot pear-shape who would be ten
with laughing bones, rapt at long, smooth
proud limbs afoot on the landscape.
Take us running, gangsters demand.
Femur, Tibia, Fibula
bold weight-lifters rising
to take control
show the 206 in full bloom.

I wish to speak
with Taliesin and Angela,
pick at their dreams.
The old world expects,
reminds me of my genealogy…
how roots wait in the dark earth
for magic's return.

Fibula, the backing-singer,
has ambitions to be front-stage,
sings aria in the bath.

The distals laugh
at over-sensitive wallowing,
wave themselves sick
but yearn to play blue-grass jazz.

ANNOUNCEMENT

This mouth is under arrest
these hands in chains,
stomach restrained.
No eating after midnight.
Only one piece of fresh fruit
permitted after 9pm – definitely
no *After Eights*.

The prisoner will agree
to any punishment deemed necessary
during the monthly contract.
There shall be no formal
apology for recent floggings.
Changes to the programme:
now everything stops for blood.

Teeth extraction will stay
as an incentive
for good behaviour
as do hand amputations.

The benefits of this system
resurrect a young, healthy body
under your control.
Permanently.

Remember, you are here
on a voluntary basis…
may leave at any time.
You would like to fit
through the door
wouldn't you?

LANDSCAPES

I found *Vosene* in the pound shop, plunged
back to the sixties, clean when my hand
squeezed rinse water off – that fresh squeak
before the conditioner operation.

The old home held a dead grandmother,
dead father, dead dog. My mother made it
to hospital and the house died alone.
Its wallpaper layers captured decades,

the deepest skin, pink emulsion, stamped leafs;
potato-art picked up my father's voice telling
tales of decorating after the war. Newspapers
under the lino; new raincoats for 19/6, corsets

like the dragon-grandmother's laid out on her bed,
talced-rubber waiting to roll around her beneath
the Paisley-patterned wrap. In the 60s, home
smelled of soup, of scones shaped like people.

A small boiler cooked the whites, and great big
clootie-dumplings in a pillow-case to be baked dry
in the oven. Cousins stayed – my mother bought
food: not ornaments and fancy rugs or posh tosh.

The air in our rooms was thick with mess, laughter...
they never wanted to go home to their glass houses.
Friends came and didn't go...the years spun
out of control. Grandchildren hung on Mum's neck

in a house that wasn't home any more. My house
is full of me, portable, already claimed to dress
grandchildrens' lives; books, shelving, bedding…
digital gadgetry, to sail up a century smelling of me.

From 11th

A new poison
after disappointment.

I count days differently
from her, have information
she wouldn't hear.

HISTORY 1

In the mood, jazz and love-struck
ballads from big Bakelite sound, toned,
rich, deep and blousy. The fifties swung.

Party's at our house, filled living-rooms –
One singer one song,
whisky men, sherry women
and when I die, don't bury me at all...
pickle her bones in alcohol.

Granny's dancing
in her wrap-around Paisley apron.
Aunty Lucy sets up to *Roll*
a silver dollar down upon the ground.
She blasts her party piece,
I'm caught, forgotten behind a chair.

Time at night goes on forever.
Aunty Mary's, *You're free to go,*
Darling, echoes through the house.

PRIZE

We act as if we know air,
call it aether, airways, heavens, sky,
say it carries waves...well it does –
wi-fi, radio, other things;
Spectres and the like.

They have a right to be here,
there, across the bloody universe
drifting figures on the clock, waiting
to loom...in war-time, race, win
a prize; which is what?

Us. I assume the appellation
for human beings in transition
on the highways up there
free of the body, unaware
of our success.

LITTLE SISTER

In-law or outlaw I can wail
at the space you'll leave.

All the supermarkets will notice
empty minutes
that might have contained you...
the world around us has already
3-D printed your laughing face.

We expect to see it as we turn
corners, catch you watching us
as we walk towards you.

WARRIOR GHOSTS

Never have to wash the blood
of battle from their hair, gouge bloody gunge
out of fingernails, worry about germs,
body odour – leaky ears.

They show up wearing Death-day clothes
leave rambling images on our air...
individuals we never knew pinned
down the years for centuries.

They don't hear us but know that we're
the walking dead, wearing hubris
on stupid heads like a floppy straw hat
in torrential rain. They're the watchmen.

OUR MULTIVERSE

The world inside the mirror
doesn't see me, know I'm here
peering in at its place in life –
it's dead, receding even from me.
Nothing remains of that moment.
Time is mashed together, frozen
so we can glance back at the décor
we chose, lived with, talked to
when everything slipped.
Pockets, jars and baskets hold
picnics, nightmares...special days,
particular food – one of mine serves
fresh dates with Marscapone cheese,
another, kids gushing through the house,
back and front doors open
me deep in a book on a sofa.
Actions have front covers
like DVDs stacked on shelves.
We are libraries and everything
depends on the librarian...
what lives again and again
what's lost because there's no assistant
or volunteer with a key or password
or hammer to break into our self.

X-RAY VISION

I'm a loose woman; bed and prison-chair
notice I'm in love with Toilet Throne –
it sees me more than the kitchen. The new
fat-busting pills beat gym rigmarole...all
that pumping of knees and starving to lose
a slob. My body squirms at sweat, snuggles
in a lounger. Will we ever move on
from this phase in evolution...and does
evacuated fat contribute to
Armageddon? The living-room throne hooks
me in, swings my feet up, keeps me well-read,
waiting for science to reach fiction, make
me see inside my body, not my head
which is lost in unknown territory.

Living in an Artefact

Sinking into a canvas, holding on
for ever to the writing on the wall;
speed-crafted letters outlined in black jab
at the world's scathing eyes that don't bother
to read. This is me, the remnant at home
with her walls, growing in a chair, a weed,
unkempt, unwanted and pestilential.
I know where everything is, extending
grabber supports my freedom to just sit
through action – exorcising exercise.
I'm in training for the long death, losing
mindfulness; living statues in tourist
season perfect this view of life, pull in
coin...live to pay the piper and the bills.

SATURDAY SEDATION

Big day in the house, people flowing; not like a river but a pool being stirred on impulse, giving way, allowing others to touch her, sit and hold her hand, make her feel part of the mixing company. When we asked her a question her eyes flickered open and she'd answer *Yes* or *No, Please* and *Thanks Doll*. Family branches tipping *Hi*, hugging. Introductions to those who missed meeting over the years; I met Betty and fell in love with Tricia's necklace fan...she let me wear it for a while. I gave Gina a turn – bought myself one on *Amazon* later that night. Nurses and doctor in and out, making her comfortable. We packed the kitchen. Bad news filtered through.

Later, painting stones, distracting young ones. Kelly and Lorraine adventured into gardens with Rihanna, to find more. I photographed their work, marked it with *Exceeds Expectations* and *Outstanding*s – only Donald and Rihanna earned an O. We laughed, cackled, cracked and taught this young granddaughter of the house how to live with death. Nine is surely too young to have that force-fed, but not really; she'll have memories, of Nana unlike Elliot and the new baby coming. Death caught Fiona at fifty-three, barely able to blow a handful of candles out two weeks previous.

At 8.30 on Sunday morning I lost a young sister-in-law, her siblings another sister, children their mother, their children, Nana. Joe is bereft without the love of his life. We all learn to live with Death as a neighbour.

YOU FLY YOU DIE

If I climb onto the kitchen counter to finally wallpaper above
the window I could tumble, live a hermit's end hidden from
letterbox eyes. Decrepitude inches up my legs and down from
the crown of my head – it may be time to wear my glasses, see
faces, sit the end out and yet I stand and stare, measure the
plan, worry about slipping on paste. Twenty-five years ago I
stood trembling on the edge of my mother's bath; I'd glossed
all the walls, realised that energy had forsaken me at forty.
Such a small strip. I could nip up there, slap it on. Both my
heads are nodding; the windows are double glazed – flight
impossible without missile-status and no room to get up speed
or weight. If I lost a stone my knees could cope – half a body
and I could fly up there in a nifty minute, slip down like a
ballerina on Valium, pirouette and take a bow. Heads are
counting, weighing time – ten years has made the strip
invisible...probably, but I could slim into the job.

MY YGGDRASIL (World Tree)

Gentleman of the garden
holding the corner, he spreads his hands
shades all through the warm year.
He offers breezy advice, footholds...
grants me living room to spend time in green light,
view the loch, unwind in his solid arms
to ponder adventure in other kingdoms.
I expect fairies as neighbours, some day.
A tree mythologist would spot hidden doors in knots –
trees are homes too. If there was a squirrel
to run out on top branches, I'd have him spear
rabble-rousing pigeons with insults...clear my roof
of their stomping. Magpies, crows, tits and jackdaws
gather, clamour in the tree, the garden, my mind.
From upstairs or tiered high in the gods
we're affiliated to the world, feel how sturdy
is the tree that also touches sky, seduces us
with aerial fascination. The spectrum holds
The Well of Being in place, fastens us to it.
We don't fly, spin into space: are firmly planted
free to experiment with devices; technology
powers our mobility to blindly pillage universes
developing in a future far far...

Lady Russet 1

All of our leaves are tinted, falling
underfoot. We tread hopefully
through rustling crackle
up-selling the space forward. Stretchable
musings and what-ifs drift around
nodding heads – we boldly wear the crown.

Vapours are lost on us; we thrust
ourselves over obstacles, with cursive
inscriptions to scribble our history…
coursing decades, adding stories
encountered by older generations
slipping now, to be standing stones.

FIONA EDMISTON WAS HERE

I took the last photo of you
laughing on the 31st
at the sight of a full-candled cake
barely two weeks ago
all lit up with the fun of it
reaching that magic number –
53 summers. You share that day
with Harry Potter. Fame at last
but partly because the stream
of silver limos that carried you away
did it on the anniversary
of Elvis's death...simple details
to put a smile on all our hearts
that hurt as the sun bursting
out of a wet August gleamed
on the stunning cars.

You were the one we didn't expect
to shine so soon like this. Your quiet
life helped you slip into a unit,
live as best you could on a branch.
The loss of you creates a hole
in the tree; we expected a bough
to break from the oldies at the top…
have been sideswiped, choked
at *Death* with his claws out.
Look at us now, reeling
with flash-memories, counting
the years we lived, all
our little branches, losing time.
Suddenly you have risen to the top –
no fairy on our tree: we have an angel.

TREE OF READY MEALS

This woman, Lily,
is long-boned, legs like skewers,
empty breasts lying
on furrows of ribs. She smiles
at guests who kiss, kiss,
planting babies in her lap.
Food appears – magic:
fish is chicken, porridge is
soup…and beautiful.
The old Lily was hidden
in layers of faded
muscle, dressed in blue-flowered
polyester sacks.
Fourteen children darted in
and out. Wives, husbands.
Grandchildren flapped hands at mince
with onion, without.
Potatoes – no potatoes,
steak pie, Spam. Fat chips:
thin. Tea, no jam. Fried liver
for William, rabbit
stew for John. Licked-clean dishes
stacked the sink, smells ran
up walls, dripped off stairs, settled
when at last she sank
into her patient armchair.
Lily, while you sleep
the imprints of last kisses
fade in the night air.
We smoothed your brow, calmed weary
hearts, and voices filled
the room with mad memories.
We laughed, the children
cried – they were confused. You slipped

out of our lives...we
counted breaths with you and breathed
in the air you left behind.

WAVING

Fiona was here, as was Jean,
Edith, Graham, William and
big Donald. Ryan was here – if
only a few minutes. Roseanne, Eric,
Fern-the-dog and Finn, Sue Roebuck
and Ruben Woolley...gone,
passed from one hand to another.
Kirk Douglas and Bowie –
famous and Hoi Polloi
walk the same path in the end.

We rise. Fi's up there, eyes closed
on a sofa swing. Stars decorate
the night, the moon screening
Elvis, but family steals the show.

Acknowledgements

LITTLE SISTER posted in *FB* Aug 2019,
FIONA EDMISTON WAS HERE published in *The Writers'
Cafe* autumn 2019
BODY LANGUAGE published *Laldy!* December 2018
BORN TOO LATE published *In Between Hangovers*
December 2017
DONOR published on *Written in a Woman's Voice* blog
17&18th Jan 2019
GOING GENTLY published *Glasgow Review of Books* June
2017
LANDSCAPES published in T*he Writers' Cafe* May 2019
NOW published by *Screech Owl*, 2015
PAPER TRAIL published *Visual Verse* May 2018
SECRET GARDENS published on *Vapour Trails* July 2018
THE WEIGHT OF GHOSTS *NorthWords Now* 2012
WHISKY THOUGHTS published *I am not a Silent Poet* June
2018
LIVING IN AN ARTEFACT published *Nine Muses* 12th May
2019
OUR MULTIVERSE published *Visual Verse* May 2019
YOU FLY YOU DIE published *Southlight* autumn 2019
LADY RUSSET 1 commended in *Autumn Voices* acrostic
comp Jan 2020
TREE OF READY MEALS pub *The Same blog* May 2018
and
nominated for the *Pushcart Prize* 2019

Black&White art on dedication page by the author
originally published in Southlight Magazine 2019

ABOUT THE WRITER

This poetry collection centres on life and how we amble into old and older age...unless death arrives to spoil the party, which it did here. A young-ish death in the middle of a huge family is always hysterical, tearful, with family members, friends, hovering, hugging, crying in corners, laughing at old tales. The story of our response to Fiona's *Triple Negative Inflammatory Breast Cancer* is sandwiched with my life, thoughts, offering a small picture of Fiona, who didn't get to beat the clock. None of us do. I didn't want to fill this book with only negatives so there are funny elements, political rants, and memoir here that should connect with everyone who has lived with difficulty. May the act of life be thunder in our ears and a swift ride on the river at the end, our fingers trailing in the water.

Irene Cunningham has been published in many poetry magazines over thirty years. Last year, she finished writing a novel...not one of the many neglected projects, no, a brand new idea that enveloped her last summer and was forcefully ejected from her head by the end of November. She's editing it now – who knows how long that will take. A new poetry collection, *Fairytale,* was published last year and is available on *Kindle* and paperback. She is retiring from her bread n butter job and can't wait to dance to her own timetable, writing or arty-crafting. https://ireneintheworld.wixsite.com/writer

Also available from *Amazon* is a poetry conversation between her and fellow poet Diana Devlin – *SANDMEN: A Space Odyssey* published by Hedgehog Press 2018, and *Halloween* a collection of poetry and prose on witchy themes.

Printed in Poland
by Amazon Fulfillment
Poland Sp. z o.o., Wrocław

54755170R00040